Las Vegas Cooks!

Recipes from popular restaurants
on the Strip, Downtown,
and across the Las Vegas Valley

All She Wrote ★ Las Vegas, Nevada

This one's for Dad.

Recipes from popular restaurants on the Strip, Downtown, and across the Las Vegas Valley

Published by
All She Wrote
4754 E. Flamingo Road, Suite 384
Las Vegas, Nevada 89121

Library of Congress Catalog Card Number: 97-73358
ISBN: 0-9658172-0-2

Publisher's Cataloging-in-Publication
Las Vegas cooks!: recipes from popular restaurants on the strip, downtown, and across the Las Vegas valley / Linda Linssen, editor. — 1st ed.
      p. cm.
Includes index.
Preassigned LCCN: 97-73358
ISBN: 0-9658172-0-2

1. Cookery—Nevada—Las Vegas. I. Linssen, Linda.

TX715.2.S69L37 1997   641.59793'135
                            QBI97-40732

Acknowledgements

I wish to extend a sincere thank you to all the Las Vegas chefs and restaurant owners who so generously shared their recipes, and to the hotel/casino general managers, restaurant support staff members, and public relations personnel who assisted in getting the recipes to me.

I am indebted to Mark Young of Young @ ART for providing the artwork and the moral support, to Larry Letourneau for being a first-class friend and my second pair of eyes, and to Nigel Linssen and Neil Linssen for sharing their mother's enthusiasm.

Also, many thanks to Ten Speed Press for use of the recipes from *Fog City Diner Cookbook* by Cindy Pawlcyn, ©1990.

Linda Linssen
Las Vegas, Nevada

Note to users of this cookbook

Las Vegas chefs hail from many regions of the world. As such, one of my editorial goals was to try to make their recipes somewhat consistent in expression (and, therefore, widely accessible) while maintaining the integrity of the chefs' own words.

In a few cases, chefs chose not to state the number of servings their recipes yield. To prepare one of those recipes at home, I recommend that you check the ingredients list for quantities of main ingredients. From those quantities, you should be able to determine an approximate yield.

Some of the ingredients or cooking terms used by professional chefs may be unfamiliar to you. For this reason, I have included a glossary on pages 118-119. If an ingredient listed is unavailable in your area, you may be able to substitute a similar ingredient and still achieve excellent results.

Throughout the book, I have used product names as provided by the chefs. Any corruption of a product name or omission of a product trademark is unintentional and not to be regarded as a reflection on the products' companies, or on the chefs who provided the product names. Whenever possible, I have included product trademarks with company permission.

Contents

"There is no love sincerer than the love of food."

—*George Bernard Shaw*

Appetizers

Scampi Appetizer

5 jumbo shrimp, peeled and deveined
3 tablespoons flour
2 tablespoons cooking oil
2 tablespoons butter
1 teaspoon pure lemon juice
1 tablespoon white wine
¼ teaspoon fresh garlic, finely chopped
4 ounces whipping cream
½ teaspoon chopped parsley

Dust shrimp with flour and place in a hot skillet with cooking oil. Turn shrimp frequently until golden brown. Drain off cooking oil and dispose. Lower heat; add butter, lemon juice, white wine, garlic, and whipping cream. Frequently shaking pan, increase heat until liquid reduces to a thick sauce. Place shrimp on a side dish. Pour sauce over shrimp and sprinkle with parsley. Serve hot.

Makes 1 serving.

Philips Supper House

"Las Vegas' Finest Dining in an Intimate Edwardian Atmosphere"

Crab Cakes

Mario S. Capone, Chef de Cuisine

Crab Cake Mix:
1 pound lump crab meat
1 egg yolk
1 stalk green onion, finely diced
2 ounces red bell pepper, finely diced
2 ounces red onion, finely diced
1 ounce fresh lemon juice
1 ounce fresh cilantro, chopped
2 ounces Aioli
Olive oil
Bread crumbs
Salt and pepper to taste

Combine all ingredients in a large bowl and mix carefully. Do not break up crab meat. (Leave in lumps.) Pack by hand into 16 cakes, using a ring. Place cakes on a sheet pan sprinkled with bread crumbs, which help with absorption.

Sauté cakes in olive oil until brown. Turn over the cakes and brown the other side. Bake in a 325-degree oven for 10 to 12 minutes.

Aioli:
18 ounces canola oil
3 egg yolks, room temperature
1 teaspoon dijon mustard
1 ounce fresh lemon juice
Salt and pepper to taste

While whisking, drizzle canola oil into egg yolks, dijon mustard, and lemon juice until thick. Season with salt and pepper.

Achiote Oil:
1 ounce achiote seeds

4 ounces canola oil
Steep achiote seeds in canola oil until oil is red in color.

Avocado Purée:
2 avocados
½ lime, juiced
Salt and pepper to taste

Mix the avocado, lime juice, and salt and pepper until smooth.

Garnished Salad:
½ red onion, julienned
½ stalk green onion, julienned
¼ bunch cilantro leaves
1 plantain, thinly sliced

Mix the red onion and green onion with a little olive oil, lemon juice, and salt and pepper. Add the cilantro. Garnish with Achiote Oil and a thinly-sliced plantain chip fried in canola oil until crisp.

Presentation:
Place the avocado purée on the bottom of the plate.
Place the crab cakes at 3 o'clock and 9 o'clock.
Place the fried plantain chip in the middle of the plate, face up.
Place garnished salad in the middle.
Garnish with olive oil and Achiote Oil around the plate.
Finish with Aioli on each crab cake.

Makes 8 servings.

Neros
Caesars Palace
"Creative American Cuisine"

Escargot Ravioli in Roasted Garlic Broth

Pierre Deruaz, Chef

24 escargot (burgundy)
Court bouillon with garlic
5 ounces julienne of leeks, carrots, and celery
1 pinch fresh tarragon, chopped
1 ounce olive oil
4 garlic cloves
1 ounce shallots, chopped
5 ounces dry white wine
5 ounces chicken stock
3 ounces heavy cream
2 ounces butter
2 teaspoons fresh parsley, chopped
24 wonton skins
1 egg yolk
½ tomato, diced

Cook the escargot in court bouillon with garlic; set aside.

Sauté the julienne of vegetables at low heat for a few minutes. Add the chopped tarragon; set aside. Peel and chop the garlic cloves. Sauté in olive oil until golden brown; set aside.

Garlic Broth:
In a saucepan, combine the chopped shallots, dry white wine, and chicken stock. Bring to a boil and reduce liquid by half. Add the heavy cream; reduce liquid slightly. Remove from heat and add butter, chopped garlic, and chopped parsley. Season and set aside.

Escargot Ravioli:
On 1 wonton skin, place 2 escargot and a pinch of julienne of vegetables. With the egg yolk, brush the outer edges of the wonton skin and place 1 other wonton on top of it. Press the edges firmly to seal; cut to size with a round cookie cutter.

Repeat the procedure with remaining wonton skins, escargot, and julienne of vegetables. (Reserve a small amount of the julienne of vegetables for garnish.) Cook the ravioli in boiling, salted water for a few minutes; drain.

Presentation:
For each serving, place 3 ravioli in a deep soup plate. Cover with the Garlic Broth. Garnish with diced tomato and reserved julienne of vegetables.

Makes 4 servings.

Renata's Le Bistro Du Vin
"An Exclusive Facility with Its Own Charm and Intimacy for Entertaining"

Pan-Seared Foie Gras with Apple Purée, Balsamic Glaze, and Roasted Hazelnuts

Jenny Muller, Entremetier

½ cup hazelnuts
2 medium Granny Smith apples, cored
2 tablespoons unsalted butter, cut into pieces
1 tablespoon brandy
1 teaspoon white wine vinegar
¼ cup balsamic vinegar
2 tablespoons Madeira wine
2 tablespoons port wine
1 tablespoon walnut oil
1 medium shallot, minced
1 teaspoon each: minced fresh tarragon, chervil, thyme,
   flat leaf parsley
Sherry vinegar
Salt and pepper to taste
10 ounces fresh duck foie gras
4 cups baby spinach leaves

Roasted Hazelnuts: Preheat oven to 400 degrees. Spread hazelnuts on small, rimmed baking sheet and toast 8 to 10 minutes, or until skins blister. Wrap hazelnuts in a kitchen towel and vigorously rub them together to remove skins. Coarsely chop the nuts. Reduce oven temperature to 350 degrees.

Apple Purée: Put apples in small baking dish and scatter pieces of butter around. Bake for about 25 minutes or until apples are tender; let cool slightly. Scoop apple pulp into a food processor. Add the apple cooking juices, the brandy, and the white wine vinegar; purée until smooth. Transfer apple purée to a small bowl; cover and keep warm.

Balsamic Glaze: In a small, nonreactive saucepan, boil balsamic vinegar, Madeira wine, and port wine over moderate heat until reduced by half; keep warm.

Sherry Vinaigrette: In medium bowl, whisk sherry vinegar with walnut oil, shallots, tarragon, chervil, thyme, and parsley. Season with salt and pepper.

Using a long, sharp knife dipped in hot water and dried, cut the foie gras crosswise into 4 equal-size, ½-inch thick slices. Heat a large skillet until very hot. Season the foie gras slices on both sides with salt and pepper. Sear over high heat, turning once, until well-browned and crisp but still pink inside, about 1 minute per side.

Presentation: Spoon the warm apple purée onto plates. Arrange the foie gras slices alongside the purée; spoon balsamic glaze over. Add the spinach leaves to the sherry vinaigrette and toss to coat. Mound the spinach leaves on the plates. Scatter the roasted hazelnuts over the foie gras and serve.

Makes 4 servings.

André's French Restaurant

Voted #1 in "Best of Las Vegas" for Most Romantic, Best Gourmet, and Best French Restaurant

Fresh Maine Lobster Carpet Bags

Timothy J. Prescott, Chef

Carpet Bag Filling:
3 ounces salted butter
2 tablespoons green onion, finely minced
1 teaspoon fresh garlic, finely minced
¼ pound poblano mushrooms, finely diced
½ pound fresh spinach, coarsely chopped
Salt and pepper to taste
5 ounces cooked Maine lobster, coarsely chopped
½ cup ricotta cheese
¼ cup parmesan cheese, finely shredded
½ cup mozzarella cheese, finely shredded
1 egg

In a large saucepan, melt the butter. Add green onion, garlic, and mushrooms. When the mushrooms are cooked, add the spinach, salt, and pepper. Cook until spinach is wilted. Remove from heat and set aside to cool.

In a medium-sized, stainless mixing bowl, add the cooked lobster, ricotta, parmesan, mozzarella, and 1 egg. Season to taste with salt and pepper; fold the ingredients together. To finish, combine with the cooled mushrooms-and-spinach mixture. Set aside.

Carpet Bag:
8 large sheets phyllo dough, cut in 6-inch x 6-inch squares
3 whole eggs, slightly beaten

With a pastry brush, coat each sheet of phyllo dough with the beaten eggs, layering 3 sheets per appetizer. Into the center of each layered dough square, spoon approximately 2 ounces of the Carpet Bag Filling. Wrap the dough around the filling, pinching at the neck. Leave approximately 1 inch at the top to fold open like a carpet bag.

Bake at 350 degrees until golden brown.

Makes 10 servings.

Creative Catering

"We Design a Variety of Fine Foods for Your Special Occasion."

The Burgundy Martini

Chilled, oversized martini glass
2 ounces Bombay Gin or Stolichnaya® Vodka
¼ ounce Chambord (raspberry liqueur)
1 fresh spiral lime twist
1 fresh raspberry

Pour Bombay Gin (or Stolichnaya® Vodka) and Chambord over ice. Stir and drain into chilled glass. Garnish with a fresh spiral lime twist and a fresh raspberry.

The Burgundy Room
Lady Luck Casino & Hotel
"Fine Dining in Elegant Surroundings"

Roasted Corn Crab Cakes

J. Jeffrey Frederick, Chef

2 pounds lump crab meat
1 cup mayonnaise
2 whole eggs
¼ cup roasted corn (from 1 medium ear)
½ cup cilantro, minced
1 tablespoon jalapeño pepper, minced
2 tablespoons bread crumbs (as a binding agent)
Seasoned bread crumbs (for coating crab cakes)
¼ cup green bell peppers, minced
¼ cup red bell pepper, minced

Pick crab free of shells; set crab meat aside. In a bowl, mix together mayonnaise, eggs, roasted corn, cilantro, and jalapeño pepper. Fold in crab meat; stir in 2 tablespoons bread crumbs as a binding agent. Spoon or pat mixture into 1- to 2-ounce balls, depending on cake sizes desired.

Coat cakes with seasoned bread crumbs. Deep-fry or pan-fry cakes until golden brown. Garnish and serve immediately.

For visual appeal, present the crab cakes on a decoratively tied corn husk, accompanied by minced red and green bell peppers, and a drizzle of curry oil. At Claudine's, the crab cakes are accompanied by three sauces: Creole Remoulade, Tabasco® Mustard, and Citrus Pico de Gallo.

Makes 10 to 20 cakes.

Claudine's Steak House
Harrah's Las Vegas

Ragout of Woodland Mushrooms in a Puff Pastry Shell with a Vodka Cream Sauce

Vodka Cream Sauce:
½ shot vodka
1 ounce whipping cream
Pinch of salt
1 ounce sweet butter

Combine vodka, whipping cream, and salt in saucepan. Add sweet butter and allow sauce to thicken. Set aside.

Ragout:
Assortment of wild mushrooms, sliced but not too thinly
½ teaspoon shallots, finely chopped
2 ounces butter
½ shot cognac
1 ounce bordelaise sauce
1 ounce whipping cream
Salt and pepper to taste
1 puff pastry shell
1 ounce Swiss cheese
Ground pepper
Chopped parsley

In a saucepan over medium heat, sauté mushrooms and shallots in 1 ounce of butter. When cooked, add cognac, bordelaise sauce, and whipping cream. Add salt and pepper to taste. Finish with 1 ounce of butter.

Spoon all ingredients into the puff pastry shell. Place on plate of Vodka Cream Sauce. Garnish with ground pepper, chopped parsley, and 1 slice of Swiss cheese.

Note: To make a bordelaise sauce, melt 1 teaspoon margarine over low heat. Add 1 small, thinly sliced onion; sauté until brown, then discard. Stir in 1 teaspoon flour. Remove from heat and stir in ¼ cup beef broth/red wine combination. Season with salt and pepper to taste. Sprinkle with parsley, minced onion, crushed bay leaves, and dried thyme leaves.

The Aristocrat

The Aristocrat

Voted "Best Gourmet Restaurant in Las Vegas" 4 Years in a Row

Toasted Brie on Semolina Bread with Roasted Tomato, Avocado Relish, and Wild Greens

Avocado Relish:
1 beefsteak tomato, sliced ½-inch thick
Olive oil
1 avocado, peeled, seeded, and diced medium
1 pinch granulated sugar
1 pinch cayenne pepper
2 tablespoons balsamic vinegar
1 pinch kosher salt

Rub beefsteak tomato with olive oil. Grill over open flame until just charred. Allow to cool. Dice into ¼-inch pieces. Mix together with avocado, granulated sugar, cayenne pepper, balsamic vinegar, and kosher salt.

Wild Greens:
½ cup mixed wild greens
½ teaspoon lemon juice
1 tablespoon olive oil
1 pinch kosher salt
1 pinch cracked black pepper

Wash greens and towel dry. Toss with lemon juice, olive oil, kosher salt, and cracked black pepper.

Brie Bread:
1 small loaf semolina bread
3 ounces brie cheese
2 tablespoons extra virgin olive oil

Slice semolina bread lengthwise in half. Brush with olive oil and grill lightly over an open flame. Remove from flame and place brie cheese on bread. Bake in oven for 3 to 4 minutes at 350 degrees. Remove bread from oven and serve open-faced. Garnish top with Avocado Relish and Wild Greens.

Makes 2 servings.

★ AMERICA ★

Chilled Prawns with Eggplant Salsa

18 medium-sized prawns, peeled and deveined
18 wafer-thin slices of pancetta (Italian-style bacon)
1 tablespoon olive oil

Wrap individual prawns in pancetta slices and rub lightly with olive oil. Broil for approximately 2 minutes on each side. Bake in a 400-degree oven until cooked through. Transfer to refrigerator to chill.

Eggplant Salsa:
1 cup small diced eggplant, peeled
1 tablespoon salt
½ cup zucchini, diced
½ cup sweet red onion, diced
½ cup red bell pepper, diced
½ cup green bell pepper, diced
½ cup yellow bell pepper, diced
½ cup virgin olive oil
½ cup chopped fennel
1 cup sliced sun-dried tomatoes
10 cloves minced garlic
¼ cup pine nuts, toasted
1 teaspoon crushed chili pepper flakes
1 tablespoon chopped basil
1 tablespoon chopped oregano
2 tablespoons chopped parsley
Lemon juice to taste
Fresh lemon for garnish

Place eggplant and salt in a bowl; toss together. Cover and let rest for 1 hour. Squeeze juice from eggplant and set aside.

In ¼ cup of the olive oil, sauté zucchini, red onion, and red, green and yellow peppers. Remove from olive oil and drain. Sauté the eggplant and fennel in the remaining ¼ cup of olive oil. Add sun-dried tomatoes. Remove from olive oil and drain. Combine the sautéed vegetables with remaining herbs and ingredients. Mix well and season with lemon juice to taste. Transfer to refrigerator to chill.

Presentation:
Place approximately ¼ cup of salsa in the center of each of 6 chilled plates. Surround the salsa on each plate with 3 grilled and chilled prawns. Garnish with fresh lemon and basil.

Makes 6 servings.

Stivali Italian Ristorante
Circus Circus Hotel/Casino/Theme Park
"A Northern Italian Experience"

"Serenely full, the epicure would say,
Fate cannot harm me, I have dined to-day."

—*Reverend Sydney Smith*

Accompaniments

Caesar Salad

2 cloves garlic
1 anchovy
2 egg yolks
2 teaspoons dijon mustard
6 ounces olive oil
1 tablespoon red wine vinegar
1 ounce lemon juice
1 teaspoon salt
1 teaspoon black pepper
1 head romaine lettuce: washed, drained, and torn
2 tablespoons parmesan cheese
½ cup croutons

Chop and mash garlic finely. Do the same with the anchovy. Place both in a stainless steel bowl along with the egg yolks and the dijon mustard. Blend the olive oil into the egg mixture, slowly and steadily, forming an emulsion. Add red wine vinegar, lemon juice, salt, and black pepper; mix well.

Toss the romaine lettuce leaves into the mixture. Place salad on a serving plate and sprinkle with parmesan cheese and croutons.

Treasure Island at the Mirage

Bouillabaisse

Joseph Mami, Chef

¼ cup butter or vegetable oil
1 teaspoon fresh garlic, minced
½ cup onion, julienned
½ cup green pepper, julienned
¼ cup red pepper, julienned
¼ cup celery, sliced
1 pound extra large shrimp, peeled and deveined
2 pounds of a firm, fresh fish
  (halibut, red snapper, or orange roughy)
3 to 4 fresh tomatoes, chopped
¼ cup black and green olives, sliced (optional)
8 ounces crab meat
12 fresh mussels
  (Discard top shell; use only bottom shell with mussel attached.)
12 fresh clams
  (Discard top shell; use only bottom shell with clam attached.)
¼ teaspoon salt
¼ teaspoon black pepper, freshly ground
¼ teaspoon curry powder
¼ teaspoon anise seeds
⅔ cup tomato sauce
½ cup sherry wine
1 teaspoon lemon juice

Heat butter in a large saucepan. Add garlic, onion, green and red peppers, celery, shrimp, and fish. Cook over low heat until shrimp and fish are just firm.

Add tomatoes, black and green olives, crab meat, mussels, clams, and all the spices. Add tomato sauce, sherry wine, and lemon juice. Simmer 5 to 7 minutes.

Presentation:
Serve equal portions. Place clams and mussels on outside edge of serving bowls for appeal.

Makes 6 to 8 servings.

Great Moments Room
Las Vegas Club Hotel & Casino
"Fine Dining in Casual Elegance"

Prime Rib Chili

Note: This is a large recipe. Adjust ingredient amounts according to the number of people to be served.

5½ pounds prime rib* beef, cut into ¼-inch x ¼-inch pieces
1½ tablespoons garlic, minced
1 ounce salad oil
4 cups green peppers, finely chopped
6 cups red onions, finely chopped
1¼ cups ground chili powder
1½ tablespoons ground cayenne pepper
1½ tablespoons ground cumin
2 tablespoons oregano, ground or leaves
2 teaspoons celery salt
2 cups flour
12 ounces beer
4 ounces tequila
4 cups au jus
3½ pounds tomatoes (½ #10 can)
4 cups water
2 cups catsup
*Substitute any beef you wish, but the better the meat, the better the chili!

In a sauté pan, brown the beef on all sides.

In a large pot, sauté red onions, garlic, and green peppers with salad oil for approximately 10 to 12 minutes. Add beef and mix well. Sauté mixture until meat is completely heated.

To the meat-and-onion mixture, add and incorporate all dry spices. Sauté 10 to 12 minutes. Add and incorporate the flour, making sure no flour spots remain.

Add all liquids but reserve 1½ cups water. (Add remaining water at the end only if needed.) Simmer chili 35 to 40 minutes and season to taste. Remove from heat and transfer to a sterile container. Cool down in an ice bath; cover and refrigerate.

Jeremiah's Steak House

"No Bells, No Whistles — A Las Vegas Tradition Since 1974"

Minestrone Soup

Paul Krummenacher, Chef

Pestata:
3 ounces unsalted butter
½ ounce minced garlic
½ ounce oregano
½ ounce basil
2 ounces parmesan cheese, grated

Combine all ingredients to make a smooth paste. Set aside.

Minestrone Soup:
2 ounces olive oil
4 ounces bacon, diced small
4 ounces yellow onion, diced
6 ounces leeks, diced
4 ounces zucchini squash, diced
2 ounces each red and green bell peppers, diced
4 ounces carrots, diced
4 ounces celery, diced
8 ounces potatoes, diced
2 ounces tomato purée
2 ounces tomato paste
1 gallon beef broth
2 ounces fresh tomato, ground
5 ounces fresh tomato, diced
2 ounces borlotti beans
4 ounces spinach, chopped
2 ounces tubetti pasta
Salt and pepper to taste

Pre-cook borlotti beans and tubetti pasta in separate pots.

In a large pot, sauté bacon in olive oil. Add onions, leeks, zucchini, and peppers; simmer for about 5 minutes. Add carrots, celery, and potatoes; simmer. Add tomato purée and tomato paste; simmer. Add beef broth; boil for 10 minutes.

Add ground and diced tomatoes, cooked beans, and Pestata. Cook 10 minutes; add spinach and tubetti pasta. Add salt and pepper to taste. Serve with grated parmesan cheese on the side.

Makes 10 servings.

The Flagship of the Boulder Strip

SHOWBOAT

Di Napoli
Showboat Hotel, Casino, and Bowling Center
"Fine Southern Italian Cuisine"

Low Fat Pomodoro

2 teaspoons garlic, chopped
3 cups tomato concassé
3 cups tomato juice
2 tablespoons fresh basil, julienned
¼ teaspoon salt
⅛ teaspoon white pepper

In a sauté pan over medium heat, lightly brown the garlic. Add the tomato concassé and sauté for 10 seconds. Add the tomato juice; simmer for approximately 30 seconds or until the sauce reaches the desired thickness. If, during simmering, the sauce reduces too much, add a little water or tomato juice and bring to a simmer. Add the basil, salt, and pepper. Taste; adjust seasonings, if necessary.

Serve over angel hair pasta, cooked al dente.

Treasure Island at the Mirage

Orecchiette al Broccolini

A. Giovanni Vancheri, Chef

Note: To prepare this recipe, adjust ingredient amounts according to personal taste and number of people to be served.

Orecchiette pasta
Broccoli tips
Pepperoncino
Garlic cloves, chopped
Extra virgin olive oil
Salt and pepper to taste

In pan of gently boiling water, cook desired amount of broccoli tips until al dente; set aside. Cut pepperoncino in half. Cook in olive oil with the chopped garlic cloves until they are blonde-colored. Add broccoli tips and a little salt. Simmer over medium heat.

Add orecchiette pasta with 3 tablespoons of water in which broccoli was cooked. Sauté all over high heat for 1 minute. Serve hot.

Café Milano
ITALIAN RISTORANTE

Gio's Café Milano
Recipient of "Best of the Best Five Star Diamond Award"

Cuban Black Bean Soup

Hilda Fonte, Chef

2 ½ pounds black beans
⅓ cup red wine vinegar
2 tablespoons dry sherry
2 cups olive oil
2 teaspoons white sugar
1 ½ pounds green peppers, chopped
1 ½ pounds white onions, chopped
2 cans whole red pimientos
½ teaspoon cumin
1 tablespoon crushed oregano
8 garlic cloves, crushed or minced
3 bay leaves
Salt to taste
Black pepper to taste

Soak beans overnight. Mix all ingredients together in a stock pot. Simmer until beans are tender.

PYRAMID CAFE

Papyrus Restaurant & Pyramid Cafe
Luxor Las Vegas

Mojo Criollo Cuban Sandwich

Hilda Fonte, Chef

Butter
Mustard
Sliced sweet pickles
Sliced ham
Sliced roast pork (from Roast Leg of Lamb recipe below)
Sliced Swiss cheese
Fresh white bread

Spread bread with butter and mustard. Top with other ingredients. Steam until cheese is melted.

Roast Leg of Lamb:
1 leg of pork (approximately 6 pounds)
1 cup juice of sour oranges
½ cup olive oil
10 garlic cloves, crushed
1 pound white onions, sliced
1 tablespoon crushed oregano
1½ teaspoons cumin
Salt and pepper

Mix together: orange juice, olive oil, garlic cloves, white onions, oregano, cumin, salt and pepper. Marinate pork in mixture for 4 hours. Cook at 185 degrees until done.

Nile Deli
Luxor Las Vegas

"Time spent in a kitchen teaches us that the simplest gifts of nature are filled with grandeur and mystery."

—*Bill Holm*

Main Dishes

Citrus Macadamia Chicken

½ cup macadamia nut oil
¼ cup fresh lime juice
2 tablespoons fresh rosemary, chopped (or 1 tablespoon dried)
1 tablespoon fresh basil, chopped (or ½ tablespoon dried)
½ teaspoon salt
¼ teaspoon white pepper
4 boneless chicken breasts, approximately 6 ounces each
Macadamia nuts
Chopped parsley

Combine macadamia nut oil, lime juice, rosemary, basil, salt, and white pepper. Marinate chicken breasts in mixture for 4 to 6 hours. Charbroil until done. Garnish with macadamia nuts and chopped parsley. Serve with rice and grilled vegetables.

Makes 4 servings.

Calypsos Restaurant
Tropicana Resort & Casino
"The Island of Las Vegas"

Chicken Marsala

Sun-dried Tomato Pesto:
1 cup sun-dried tomatoes
½ cup whole black olives
2 teaspoons garlic, chopped
1 tablespoon fresh rosemary (or ½ teaspoon dried)
⅛ cup olive oil

Put all Sun-dried Tomato Pesto ingredients into a food processor and purée. Set aside. (Freeze leftover pesto for later use.)

Chicken Marsala:
2 boneless, skinless whole chicken breasts, or 4 halves
2 tablespoons olive oil
½ cup flour, seasoned with salt and pepper
1 cup crimini mushrooms, sliced
½ cup Marsala wine
2 tablespoons Sun-dried Tomato Pesto
1 cup chicken stock
2 tablespoons butter, softened

In a sauté pan, heat olive oil. Dredge chicken breasts in seasoned flour; sauté in olive oil until chicken is brown on both sides and cooked through. Remove from pan and keep warm.

Add crimini mushrooms; sauté for a few minutes. Add Marsala wine; simmer until liquid is reduced by half. Add Sun-dried Tomato Pesto and chicken stock. Bring to a boil and cook until liquid is slightly reduced. Add softened butter. Cook until well-blended. Turn off heat.

Present 2 half-breasts per person. Cover each with half of sauce. Serve with rice pilaf or your favorite pasta.

Makes 2 servings.

Pastina's Italian Bistro
Four Queens Hotel & Casino
"The Best-Kept Secret in Las Vegas!"

Rosemary Chicken Pasta

Roland August, Chef

6 ounces chicken breast strips
1 tablespoon olive oil
½ teaspoon garlic, minced
3 ounces mushrooms, quartered
2 ounces sun-dried tomatoes
White wine to taste
2 sprigs fresh rosemary, minced
Salt and pepper to taste
5 ounces heavy cream
3 to 4 ounces parmesan cheese
1 tablespoon small peas
8 ounces fettuccine, cooked al dente

Sauté chicken strips in olive oil and minced garlic. Add mushrooms and sun-dried tomatoes. Add white wine. Sauté chicken until brown. Add rosemary, salt, pepper, and heavy cream. Stir in parmesan cheese and small peas. Add more cheese or more cream to reach desired consistency. (Sauce should be a little thick.) Serve over fettuccine, cooked al dente.

Makes 1 serving.

Melrose Restaurant

"Eclectic Menu Featuring Authentic Foods from around the World"

Pollo Antonio

Avocado Spread:
1 ripe avocado
¼ cup sour cream
1 teaspoon cilantro, finely chopped
½ teaspoon fresh garlic, finely chopped
½ teaspoon grated parmesan cheese
1 teaspoon Cholula™ hot sauce
Juice of ½ lime

Mash all ingredients into a fine, smooth paste. Set aside.

Pollo Antonio:
8 3- to 3½-ounce chicken breasts
Salt and pepper to taste
Garlic to taste
Vegetable oil or butter
4 flour tortillas, fried crisp
⅓ cup salsa verde (green salsa)
8 teaspoons Avocado Spread
1 tomato, sliced
1 cup Monterey Jack cheese, shredded

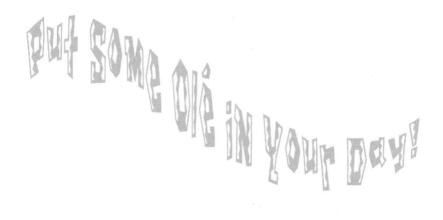

With a rolling pin or mallet, flatten chicken breasts until they are ¼-inch thin. Season with salt, pepper, and garlic. Sauté in vegetable oil or butter. Set aside.

Spread tortillas with a little salsa verde. Put Avocado Spread on top of chicken. Place 2 chicken breasts on each tortilla. Place 2 thin tomato slices on top of chicken. Sprinkle shredded cheese over tomato, partially covering the chicken.

Place in oven, set to broiler temperature. Watch closely so the cheese will melt and lightly brown without burning. Serve with Mexican rice and fresh, steamed vegetables or refried beans.

Makes 4 servings.

Ricardo's Mexican Restaurant
"Eat, Drink, and Be Mariachi!®"

Thai Me Up, Thai Me Down

8 ounces chicken breast, diced
1 ounce peanut oil
Garlic to taste
4 Thai chilies, diced
2 ounces sherry
½ teaspoon fresh mint, chopped
½ teaspoon fresh ginger, chopped
2 ounces yellow onion, diced
2 ounces red bell pepper, diced
2 ounces garlic black bean sauce
2 ounces chicken stock

Place peanut oil, garlic, and Thai chilies in pan over high heat. Sauté until garlic begins to brown. Add chicken; sauté until chicken turns white.

Deglaze with sherry; flambé. Add fresh mint and fresh ginger. After 30 seconds, add yellow onions and red bell peppers. Add black bean sauce and chicken stock. Let simmer for at least 3 minutes, stirring all ingredients. Serve over jasmine rice.

Makes 1 serving.

The Garlic Cafe
"Not Just Great Garlic — Great Food. Live, Love, and Eat Garlic!"

Club Metropolitan Chicken

Carlo Celeste, Chef

2 boneless, skinless chicken breasts
Flour
2 teaspoons shallots, chopped
2 tablespoons butter or margarine
2 small handfuls fresh spinach
White pepper to taste
3 ounces coconut creme liqueur
¾ cup heavy cream
½ cup chicken broth
8 ounces fettuccine

Dredge chicken breasts in flour and place in sauté pan, meat-side-down. Add chopped shallots; sauté in butter or margarine over high heat until chicken breasts are golden brown.

Turn over the chicken breasts and top with fresh spinach and white pepper. Sauté until back sides of chicken breasts are golden brown, about 1 minute.

Add coconut creme liqueur; flambé. Add heavy cream and chicken broth. Lower heat; simmer until liquids combine and form a gravy. Serve over fettuccine, cooked al dente.

Makes 2 servings.

The
SAFARI
Club
An
Adventure
in Eating

The Safari Club
"An Adventure in Eating!"

Chicken Angelo

3 boneless, skinless chicken breasts
Flour
Clarified butter
Dash oregano
Salt and pepper to taste
⅓ cup dry white wine
Juice of ½ to 1 small lemon
2 garlic cloves, minced
½ cup chicken broth
1 cup mushrooms, sliced
6 quartered artichoke hearts (canned or frozen)
1 tablespoon chopped parsley

Cut chicken breasts into quarters. Dredge in flour; shake off excess. In large skillet over medium heat, melt ¼ cup clarified butter. Add chicken pieces and brown all sides. Add oregano. Season with salt and pepper to taste. Add white wine, lemon juice, garlic, chicken broth, mushrooms, artichoke hearts, and parsley. Sauté over high heat until sauce thickens, stirring constantly. Serve at once.

Makes 6 servings.

Philips Supper House

"Las Vegas' Finest Dining in an Intimate Edwardian Atmosphere"

Garlic and Lemon Chicken

Michael Parker, Chef

1 cup olive oil
3 teaspoons lemon juice
½ chicken, divided into 3 sections
   (1 breast, 1 thigh, 1 drumstick)
2 whole lemons
1 cup white wine
5 cloves garlic
1 cup veal stock
1 ounce unsalted butter
Salt and pepper
Roasted garlic cloves
1 teaspoon chopped chives

Mix the olive oil and lemon juice together in a bowl. Place the chicken pieces in the mixture and refrigerate for 6 hours. Remove the chicken and brown it in a frying pan. When the chicken is golden brown, squeeze 1 lemon into the pan with the white wine and garlic cloves. Bake in a 380-degree oven for 20 minutes.

Remove chicken from the oven. Add the veal stock and simmer until reduced by half. Slowly add the butter. Peel the rind from the remaining lemon. Cut the rind into strips and blanch them in water. Cut the lemon into segments. Place the chicken in a serving bowl and pour the sauce over. Garnish with a lemon rind, lemon segments, roasted garlic cloves, and chopped chives.

Makes 1 serving.

Gallagher's Steak House
New York New York Hotel & Casino
"Prime Rib, Aged to Perfection, and Mesquite Grilled to Your Taste!"

Stuffed Shrimp (Galveston Bay Style)

Steve Willis, Chef

Sautéed Shrimp:
2 pounds jumbo shrimp
1 tablespoon margarine
1 tablespoon lemon juice
⅛ teaspoon salt
⅛ teaspoon pepper

Peel shrimp, leaving the tails on. Split each one halfway through, lengthwise down the back. Spread into a butterfly shape.

In a heavy metal saucepan, melt the margarine. Add lemon juice, salt, and pepper. Add the shrimp; sauté over low heat until pink.

Transfer shrimp to a plate to cool. Add salt and pepper to the drippings in the sauce pan.

Stuffing:
3 tablespoons margarine
1 large onion, finely chopped
½ medium-sized green bell pepper, finely chopped
2 green onions, finely chopped
2 sprigs parsley, finely chopped
1 stalk celery, finely chopped
⅓ cup day-old bread pieces, ¼-inch diced
1 pound crab meat
1 pinch cayenne pepper
2 eggs, beaten

1 pound raw shrimp: peeled, drained, and chopped
Salt and pepper to taste
1½ cups fine bread crumbs
Juice of ½ lemon

In a skillet, melt 2 tablespoons of the margarine. Add the onion, bell pepper, green onions, parsley, and celery. Simmer until vegetables are limp. Add the day-old bread pieces alternately with the beaten eggs. Add the crab meat and shrimp. Season mixture to taste with the cayenne, salt, and pepper. Remove from heat and allow to cool.

After the mixture cools, stir in the reserved drippings from the sautéed shrimp. Mound some of this mixture on the sliced side of each shrimp. Dip the entire shrimp in the bread crumbs. Place the shrimp in a well-greased baking pan and dot with the remaining margarine.

Bake at 325 degrees for 10 minutes. Turn each shrimp over and bake for another 5 minutes or until shrimp are golden brown. Sprinkle with lemon juice before serving.

Makes 6 servings.

Stockyard Steak and Seafood House
Texas Station Gambling Hall & Hotel
"In the Best Texas Tradition"

Pan Roasted Chilean Seabass with Gran Ardeche Chardonnay, 25-Year-Old Balsamic Butter, Roasted Macadamia Nuts, & Gremolada Cous Cous

Terence Fong, Chef

Chilean Seabass:
1 9-ounce Chilean seabass
2 tablespoons grapeseed oil (or oil of your choice)
Salt and pepper to taste
¼ cup Chardonnay wine
3 tablespoons 25-year-old balsamic vinegar
   (or balsamic vinegar of your choice)
2 tablespoons whole butter
1 tablespoon roasted macadamia nuts

In medium-sized pan, heat oil. Season seabass with salt and pepper. Place in hot pan. Brown 1 side, then place in oven at 375 degrees for 12 minutes.

Remove seabass from oven. Deglaze pan with Chardonnay wine and simmer until liquid is reduced by half. Add balsamic vinegar. Continue cooking until liquid is again reduced by half. Add butter. To serve, sprinkle sauce and macadamia nuts over seabass.

Gremolada Cous Cous:
2¼ cups cous cous
2¼ cups water
½ teaspoon salt

2 tablespoons butter or margarine
Zest of ½ garlic clove, minced
½ teaspoon zest of lemon and lime
½ teaspoon chopped parsley

In medium-sized pan, bring water to a boil. Add salt (optional), butter or margarine, and garlic zest. Stir in cous cous; cover. Remove from heat and let stand for 5 minutes. Add parsley; fluff cous cous lightly with fork before serving.

Note: For added flavor, substitute chicken, beef, or vegetable broth for the water.

Serve Pan Roasted Chilean Seabass with Gremolada Cous Cous, seasonal vegetables, and zest of lemon and lime.

Makes 1 serving.

Gatsby's
MGM Grand Hotel & Casino
"Setting a New Standard for a Special Blend
of the Finest Euro-Asian Cuisine"

Shrimp Thesaloniki

Niki Messologitis, Chef

6 tablespoons extra virgin olive oil
6 cloves garlic
¼ cup white wine
20 Italian plum tomatoes, diced
¼ teaspoon salt
¼ teaspoon black pepper, freshly ground
½ teaspoon fresh oregano, chopped
16 large shrimp, peeled and deveined
1 pound feta cheese, crumbled
2 teaspoons fresh basil, chopped

In a large saucepan, heat olive oil. Before smoke becomes visible, remove pan from heat and add garlic and white wine. Place pan back on heat and add diced tomatoes, salt, black pepper, and oregano. Cook over medium heat for approximately 20 minutes.

Increase heat to high and bring sauce to a boil. Add shrimp to sauce and simmer for 3 minutes. Remove sauce from heat. Add feta cheese and top with fresh basil. Cover saucepan and allow feta cheese to melt over top of sauce for 2 minutes. Pour sauce over linguini or angel hair pasta. Serve hot.

Note: Smaller portions may be served as an appetizer.

Makes 4 servings.

Café Nicolle

"Local notables, visiting dignitaries, and tired tourists seeking the utmost in continental cuisine and atmosphere have made Café Nicolle a must!"

Pecan Crusted Walleye Pike

Sergio D. Meza, Chef

½ cup RITZ® crackers, crushed
1 cup pecans, chopped
2 teaspoons garlic powder
2 teaspoons onion powder
2 teaspoons seasoned salt
1 10- to 12-ounce walleye pike fillet, boned
2 fresh eggs, beaten
1 cup vegetable oil
1 cup all-purpose flour
2 fresh lemon slices
¼ teaspoon fresh parsley, chopped

In a bowl, mix flour, RITZ® crackers, pecans, and spices. In a sauté pan, heat the vegetable oil at medium high. Brush the walleye pike fillet with beaten egg. Sprinkle with the pecan-and-cracker mixture, making sure to cover both sides well. Fry the fillet, with the skin side up first, for about 4 minutes. Turn over the fillet and cook for about 4 more minutes.

Note: Be careful not to burn the pecans!

Drain excess oil. Garnish with parsley and lemon slices. Serve with a wild rice blend and green beans with caramelized pearl onions.

Makes 1 serving.

Draft House Barn & Casino
"Midwestern-Style Cuisine in a Wisconsin Dining Experience"

Roasted Salmon in a Sliced Almond and Cracked Black Pepper Crust with Creole Mustard Béarnaise Sauce

Randy Mart, Chef

Creole Mustard Béarnaise Sauce:
1 tablespoon tarragon
¼ cup tarragon vinegar
1 tablespoon shallots, diced
Hollandaise sauce
2 teaspoons Creole mustard (mustard with red pepper sauce)

In a small saucepan, combine tarragon, tarragon vinegar, and shallots. Cook over low heat until liquid is reduced; let cool. Stir into a basic hollandaise sauce (See Note). Add Creole mustard and blend well.

Roasted Salmon:
½ cup sliced almonds
½ cup bread crumbs
1 tablespoon cracked black pepper
4 6-ounce salmon fillets
Flour
6 large eggs
2 tablespoons salad oil

Mix together almonds, bread crumbs, and cracked black pepper. Lightly dust salmon with flour. Whip eggs; dip salmon fillets in egg mixture. Roll fillets in the almonds/bread crumbs/black pepper mixture.

Heat salad oil in pan over medium heat. Sauté salmon on both sides until lightly brown. Bake in oven at 350 degrees for 12 to 15 minutes or until salmon flakes from a fork. Spread Creole Mustard Béarnaise Sauce on plate and place salmon on top. Serve hot.

Note: To make a basic hollandaise sauce, vigorously stir together 3 egg yolks and 1 tablespoon lemon juice in a medium saucepan. Add ¼ cup butter and cook over low heat, stirring constantly. Add another ¼ cup butter and continue stirring vigorously until butter melts and sauce is thick. Yields approximately ¾ cup sauce.

Makes 4 servings.

BOISON'S
RESTAURANT

Boison's Restaurant
"Continental Cuisine with French and Italian Specialties"

Grilled, Marinated Prawns with Tamari Glaze, Mango Salsa, and Zaru Soba Noodles

Terence Fong, Chef

Tamari Glaze:
3 ounces Tamari soy sauce
1 cup plum wine
½ cup simple syrup

In small saucepan, combine all ingredients. Bring to a boil. Lower the heat and simmer until reduced to a syrup consistency. Remove from heat and set aside.

Zaru Soba Noodles:
4 ounces zaru soba noodles (buckwheat noodles)
Red peppers, yellow peppers, and asparagus, julienned to yield
   ¼ cup total
1 tablespoon grapeseed oil
1 tablespoon Ajipon (citrus soy)

In a small pot, bring water to a boil. Cook noodles in water until al dente; strain. Stir-fry peppers and asparagus in grapeseed oil. Add noodles, then Ajipon. Place in center of plate.

Mango Salsa:
½ mango, peeled and diced
1 tablespoon cilantro, chopped
¼ teaspoon red Anaheim peppers
1 tablespoon lime juice
¼ teaspoon grated Hawaiian ginger
¼ tablespoon red onion, chopped

Combine all ingredients and set aside for 1 hour.

Grilled, Marinated Prawns:
3 Hawaiian, farm-raised prawns
1 tablespoon grapeseed oil
Salt and white pepper to taste

Grill prawns and place on bed of noodles. Drizzle Tamari Glaze on edge of plate and over prawns.

Garnish:
Chop pansies and sprinkle with salt and white pepper. Drizzle grapeseed oil over pansies. Place mixture on top of noodles. Serve with Mango Salsa and julienned summer vegetables.

Makes 1 serving.

Gatsby's
MGM Grand Hotel & Casino
"Setting a New Standard for a Special Blend
of the Finest Euro-Asian Cuisine"

Shellfish and Pasta Piri Piri

Piri Piri Base:
1½ cups olive oil
4 fresh jalapeño peppers, coarsely chopped
2 fresh poblano peppers, coarsely chopped
1 tablespoon crushed red pepper
1 teaspoon salt
1 tablespoon garlic, minced
8 turns freshly ground black pepper

In a saucepan over high heat, combine all ingredients except garlic. Cook, stirring, until jalapeño and poblano peppers are tender. Add garlic and let cool. Pulse in food processor until mixed but not smooth. Keep bottled at room temperature for 7 days before using.

Shellfish and Pasta:
6 clams
8 mussels
1 tablespoon olive oil
6 jumbo shrimp
½ cup chorizo sausage
2 cups shrimp stock
½ teaspoon garlic, minced
1 teaspoon shallot, minced
3 tablespoons Piri Piri Base
½ cup lobster tail meat, diced
4 ounces hand-cut noodles
Salt and white pepper to taste
Green onion, shaved (optional)

In a hot saucepan, heat clams and mussels in olive oil until they begin to open. Add shrimp, chorizo sausage, shrimp stock, garlic, shallot, Piri Piri Base, and lobster. Simmer until seafood is almost cooked through. Season to taste with salt and white pepper.

Cook pasta in boiling, salted water until tender. Toss with olive oil, salt, and pepper. Place noodles in center of bowl. Pour all ingredients over pasta. Garnish with shaved green onion.

Makes 1 serving.

Emeril's New Orleans Fish House
MGM Grand Hotel & Casino
"A New Way to Eat New Orleans Seafood"

Orange Roughy Francese

Marc Weigel, Chef

6 8-ounce boneless orange roughy fillets
6 tablespoons flour
2 whole eggs, beaten
3 ounces olive oil
1½ tablespoons shallots, chopped
1 ounce basil, chopped
Juice of 2 lemons
2 ounces white wine
5 tablespoons sweet butter, room temperature
Salt to taste
1 tablespoon parsley, chopped
1 fresh lemon

Wash orange roughy fillets under cold water. Pat dry with a paper or kitchen towel. Dip fillets in flour, then in beaten eggs. Heat olive oil in a skillet and carefully cook fillets until golden brown on both sides (approximately 2 minutes each side on medium heat). Arrange fillets on a platter.

In the skillet, add shallots and basil. Sauté; then add lemon juice and white wine. Reduce liquid by ⅔. Add butter slowly and swirl the bottom until the sauce thickens without boiling. Add salt to taste. Pour sauce over fillets. Garnish with chopped parsley and fresh lemon wedges.

Makes 6 servings.

San Lorenzo Room
Texas Station Gambling Hall & Hotel
"The Best Italian Restaurant in the Southwest"

Kiefer's Catch

1½ pounds orange roughy fillets
½ pound snow crab meat
¼ pound butter
1 teaspoon tarragon
¼ cup green onions, sliced
Puff pastry
1 ounce cheddar cheese, shredded
1 ounce Monterey Jack cheese, shredded
Egg wash

Poach orange roughy fillets; drain and cool.

Sauté snow crab meat in butter and tarragon. Add sliced green onions. Continue to sauté until most of the liquid is reduced; cool.

Heat oven to 500 degrees. On ½ sheet of puff pastry (10x16 inches), arrange 4 ounces of orange roughy. Top with 2 ounces of the crab mixture. Top with cheddar and Monterey Jack cheese. Brush surrounding pastry with egg wash. Fold over, pressing around seafood mixture. Cut around the mound to create a fish-shaped pastry. Brush with egg wash. Bake for 12 to 15 minutes.

Makes 2 servings.

Kiefer's Atop the Carriage House
"A Room with a View"

Salmon Tartare with Caviar, Fresh Dill, and Cucumber Aspic

Gerard Vullien, Maitre Cuisinier De France

12 ounces fillet of salmon
1 ounce beluga caviar

Marinate:
2 ounces gravel sugar
5 ounces kosher salt
Black pepper to taste
Fresh dill, chopped
2 tablespoons aquavit

Mix gravel sugar, kosher salt, black pepper, and fresh dill. Add aquavit. Cover the salmon fillet with the mixture and marinade for 48 hours.

Cucumber Aspic:
1 cucumber
Black pepper, salt, and cayenne to taste
Fresh dill, chopped
2 ounces whipping cream
5 ounces cucumber juice
2 tablespoons champagne vinegar
1 gelatin leaf

Peel the cucumber and dice into brunoise. Season with black pepper, salt, and cayenne. Fold in fresh dill, whipping cream, cucumber juice, and champagne vinegar.

Heat the cucumber "centrifuge." Add the gelatin leaf; stir until dissolved. Taste and adjust with the black pepper, salt, and cayenne.

Presentation:
Wash the salmon; chop to medium size and place in a circle at the center of the plate. Add ⅔ of the salmon tartare. Finish with cucumber-and-cream brunoise. Add beluga caviar for garnish.

Makes 4 servings.

PALACE COURT

Palace Court
Caesars Palace
"1996 Winner of the DiRona Award"

Seafood Linguine

1 ounce olive oil
4 jumbo shrimp
1 6-ounce lobster tail, chopped
2 green shell mussels
2 ounces fresh garlic, chopped
1 ounce champagne
4 ounces heavy cream
1 ounce salt
1 ounce pepper
1 ounce fresh lemon juice
1 ounce chives, chopped
1 ounce butter
8 ounces linguine

Heat olive oil in sauté pan. Sauté shrimp, chopped lobster, and shell mussels with the fresh garlic until seafood is halfway cooked. Add champagne and heavy cream; reduce liquid until sauce is semi-thick. Add fresh lemon juice and chives; finish with butter.

Cook linguine until al dente. Pour sauce over linguine to serve.

Makes 2 servings.

Papamios Italian Kitchen
Sam's Town Hotel & Gambling Hall
"Where Locals Eat Italian Food"

Shrimp Sauté, Tarragon, and Tomato Butter

Robert Ruegg, Chef

Tomato Butter:
1 can Italian plum tomatoes
½ teaspoon fresh thyme
¼ teaspoon fresh marjoram
1 dash cayenne pepper
3 pounds butter, unsalted

Blend all ingredients thoroughly.

Shrimp Sauté:
4 jumbo shrimp
1 ounce olive oil
½ ounce shallots, chopped
1 teaspoon fresh tarragon
½ fresh tomato, diced
1 ounce chablis wine
2 ounces fish stock
1 teaspoon Tomato Butter

Sauté shrimp in olive oil, about 2 minutes. Add shallots, tarragon, and tomatoes. Deglaze with chablis wine and fish stock for 1 minute. Finish with Tomato Butter.

Makes 4 servings.

Seasons Restaurant
Bally's Las Vegas
"Exclusive Fine Dining"

Blackened Whitefish

1 tablespoon sweet paprika
2 ½ teaspoons salt
1 teaspoon onion powder
1 teaspoon garlic powder
1 teaspoon cayenne
¾ teaspoon white pepper
¾ teaspoon black pepper
½ teaspoon dried thyme leaves
½ teaspoon dried oregano leaves
½ cup melted butter
6 orange roughy fillets, approximately 8 to 10 ounces each

Heat a large cast iron skillet over very high heat until it is beyond the smoking stage and you see white ash in the skillet bottom, at least 10 minutes. (The skillet cannot be too hot for this dish.)

Thoroughly combine seasonings in a small bowl. Dip each fillet in melted butter so that both sides are well-coated. Sprinkle seasoning mix generously and evenly on both sides of the fillets, patting it in by hand. Place fillets in the hot skillet and pour 1 teaspoon melted butter over each. (Be careful, as the butter may flame up.) Cook, uncovered, over the same high heat until the fillets' undersides look charred, about 2 minutes. The time will vary according to the fillets' thickness and the heat of the skillet.

Turn the fillets over. Again, pour 1 teaspoon melted butter on top. Cook until fillets are done, about 2 minutes. Repeat with remaining fillets. Serve hot.

Makes 6 servings.

Philips Supper House
"Las Vegas' Finest Dining in an Intimate Edwardian Atmosphere"

Sautéed Scallops with Macadamia Nuts

Pui Hui, Chef

Natural Sauce:
1 ounce chicken broth
¼ teaspoon chicken powder
⅛ teaspoon sugar
½ teaspoon cornstarch

Mix all of the Natural Sauce ingredients together. Set aside.

Sautéed Scallops:
6 ounces scallops
1 ounce celery, diced
1 ounce straw mushrooms, sliced
1 ounce bamboo shoots
1 ounce carrots, diced
4 ounces macadamia nuts, diced
Fresh ginger root, sliced

Cook the scallops, vegetables, and macadamia nuts in a high-heat wok with ginger root in the Natural Sauce. Serve hot.

Makes 2 servings.

EMPRESS COURT

Empress Court
Caesars Palace
"Finest Gourmet Chinese in Las Vegas"

Shrimp Scampi

24 medium shrimp, peeled and deveined
1 ounce olive oil
2 tablespoons garlic, chopped
2 tablespoons shallots, chopped
3 ounces white wine
1 ounce lemon juice
½ pound solid butter, cut into small pieces
3 teaspoons tomato concassé
3 teaspoons scallions, thinly sliced
1 teaspoon fresh basil, julienned
¼ teaspoon salt
⅛ teaspoon white pepper

In a large sauté pan over medium heat, sauté shrimp in olive oil for approximately 1 minute. Turn over the shrimp and sauté the other side. Add the garlic and sauté for 10 seconds. Add the shallots and sauté for another 10 seconds.

Deglaze the pan with white wine and lemon juice. Remove the shrimp from the pan and place on a plate to reserve.

Allow the liquid to reduce until about 1 tablespoon remains. Reduce the heat to low and slowly whisk the butter pieces into the liquid to emulsify and become creamy in consistency.

Note: Butter must be kept moving in the pan to avoid melting. If the heat is too high, the butter will melt rather than emulsify. If this happens, remove the pan from the heat, add a drop of water to recover the creamy consistency, and continue to whisk in the butter.

When the butter is incorporated, add the tomato concassé, scallions, basil, salt, and white pepper. Reintroduce the shrimp and heat for about 45 seconds, or until hot. Adjust salt and white pepper to taste.

Makes 1 serving.

Treasure Island at the Mirage

Vermicelli Ristorante Ju Ju Mare

2 ounces olive oil
4 whole baby artichoke hearts
1 teaspoon shallots, chopped
4 whole extra large shrimp, chopped
4 teaspoons prosciutto ham, chopped
1 cup spring mix lettuce
4 ounces chicken stock
4 teaspoons butter
2 teaspoons fresh basil, rough cut
Salt and pepper to taste
6 ounces vermicelli, cooked al dente

Heat olive oil in skillet. Add the artichoke hearts and shallots; sauté for 2 minutes on low heat. Add the shrimp; sauté until half-cooked, about 2 minutes. Add the prosciutto ham. Add the spring mix lettuce; sauté just until the lettuce starts to wilt. Add chicken stock; simmer until liquid is reduced by half. Add butter and fresh basil. Adjust salt and pepper to taste.

Toss in the hot vermicelli. Garnish with a fresh basil cluster.

Makes 2 main course servings or 4 appetizer servings.

Ristorante Italiano
Riviera Hotel & Casino
"Recognized As One of the Premiere
Las Vegas Dining Spots for over a Decade!"

Escargot Roquefort over Angel Hair Pasta, with Toasted Almonds

Georges La Forge, Chef

24 escargot
1 tablespoon butter
½ teaspoon garlic, crushed
⅓ cup cognac
½ cup white wine
½ cup clam juice
1 cup whipping cream
2 ounces roquefort cheese
4 ounces angel hair pasta
Toasted, sliced almonds
Chopped parsley

Wash escargot and sauté in butter. Add the garlic; sauté lightly. Flambé with the cognac. Add the white wine; reduce liquid. Add the clam juice; reduce liquid. Finish with the whipping cream and roquefort. Continue to reduce liquid until sauce is thick.

Cook the angel hair pasta; drain and pour into individual dishes. Pour sauce over the pasta. Garnish with toasted almonds and chopped parsley.

Makes 6 servings.

Pamplemousse
"A French Restaurant with a Romantic Country Atmosphere"

Salmon Scampi Embers

Stephan Harlan & Dan Schoen, Chefs

Scampi Butter:
2½ ounces butter
½ ounce garlic
Parsley

Mix ingredients thoroughly.

Salmon Scampi:
3 ounces Scampi Butter
1 ounce celery, chopped
1 ounce red onion, diced
1 ounce mushroom buttons, sliced
7 ⅛-inch pieces of artichoke crown
1 ounce fresh tomato, diced
2 ounces sauterne wine
8 ounces fresh salmon
Dash of worcestershire sauce
Dash of Tabasco® Pepper Sauce
Dash of salt
Dash of lemon juice
4 dashes white pepper
Saffron rice

IMPERIAL PALACE
HOTEL & CASINO • LAS VEGAS, NEVADA

Melt Scampi Butter in saucepan. Add celery, red onion, mushroom buttons, and artichoke crown; sauté 2 minutes. Add tomato and sauterne wine; simmer 1 minute. Add salmon, worcestershire sauce, Tabasco® Pepper Sauce, salt, lemon juice, and white pepper. Cook until salmon is done, about 2 minutes. Serve over saffron rice. Garnish plate with arugula leaf, tomato wedge, lemon wedge, and watercress, if desired.

Makes 2 servings.

Embers Restaurant
Imperial Palace Hotel & Casino

Swordfish Chop al Fresco

Henry Jones, Chef

Marinade for 12 to 15 chops:
(Adjust according to number to be served.)
4 cups olive oil
4 ounces lemon juice
4 ounces basil
3 tablespoons minced garlic

Mix together all ingredients and pour over swordfish. Marinate in refrigerator overnight.

Swordfish:
1 10-ounce, center-cut swordfish
2 ounces olive oil
1 teaspoon minced garlic
4 ounces roma tomato concassé
1 pinch oregano
1 pinch crushed red pepper
5 leaves fresh basil
1 ounce white wine
2 ounces clam juice
1 pinch salt and pepper

Broil marinated swordfish until just done. Heat sauté pan and add olive oil. Sauté garlic until slightly browned. Add roma tomato concassé, oregano, crushed red pepper, and basil.

Deglaze with white wine. Add clam juice and reduce liquid slightly. Add salt and pepper. Spoon sauce onto plate. Place swordfish on top. Garnish as desired and serve hot.

Makes 1 serving.

Pasta Pirate
California Hotel & Casino
"Traditional Homestyle Pasta Dishes
and Fresh Seafood Prepared Before Your Very Eyes!"

Fresh Salmon with Honey Mustard Sauce

Georges La Forge, Chef

8 ounces honey
2 tablespoons whole grain mustard
Juice of ½ lemon
¼ teaspoon garlic, crushed
2 tablespoons butter
4 8-ounce salmon steaks
½ cup white wine

Combine honey, mustard, and lemon juice; set aside. Mix garlic into butter; set aside.

Lay the salmon steaks in a baking dish. Pour the honey-mustard mixture over them. Add white wine. Top each salmon steak with the butter/garlic mixture. Bake 15 minutes at 350 degrees.

Remove the salmon steaks with a spatula. Spoon the honey-mustard sauce over each one.

Makes 4 servings.

Pamplemousse
"A French Restaurant with a Romantic Country Atmosphere"

Coconut Fried Shrimp with Chutney Mango Sauce

Chutney Mango Sauce:
5-ounce jar chutney
2 fresh mangoes, finely diced

Blend chutney for 30 seconds. Gently stir in mangoes.

Coconut Fried Shrimp:
1 pound large shrimp
4 ounces coconut milk
4 ounces all-purpose flour
4 ounces cornstarch
2 eggs yolks
12 ounces beer
1 pinch white pepper
8 ounces coconut flakes

Butterfly shrimp. Soak in coconut milk; set aside. In medium bowl, mix the following to make a batter: flour, cornstarch, egg yolks, beer, and white pepper. Dip soaked shrimp into batter, then into coconut flakes. Deep fry until golden brown. Serve with Chutney Mango Sauce.

Note: To butterfly shrimp, remove heads and shells but not tails. Slice shrimp deeply, almost to underside. Remove vein and press shrimp open to resemble a butterfly.

Makes 1 to 2 servings.

Oasis Coffee Shop
Aladdin Hotel & Casino
"A Gourmet Delight, Morning or Night"

Salmon en Croûte á la Aristocrat

8 to 10 ounces fresh Norwegian salmon fillet
Dry white wine
1 ounce shallots, finely chopped
Salt and freshly ground pepper to taste
½ cup whipping cream
Puff pastry dough
Egg wash
3 ounces shrimp
1 ounce fresh crab meat
1 ounce butter
Fresh chives and lemon wedges for garnish

The Aristocrat

Poach the salmon in dry white wine. Add shallots. Add salt and pepper to taste. Add whipping cream; reduce liquid until thick. Remove salmon fillets from sauce.

Wrap salmon fillets in puff pastry dough. Form dough into the shape of a fish; brush with eggwash. Bake in a 375-degree oven for 7 to 10 minutes or until fillets are golden brown.

Add shrimp and crabmeat to the sauce. Simmer for 10 minutes.

Presentation:
Spoon sauce onto a plate. Place salmon on top of sauce. Garnish with fresh chives and lemon wedges.

Makes 1 serving.

The Aristocrat
Voted "Best Gourmet Restaurant in Las Vegas" 4 Years in a Row

Lobster Cognac

John P. Muccio, Chef

1 4- to 6-ounce lobster tail
Flour
1 tablespoon olive oil
1 teaspoon shallots
3 to 4 fresh basil leaves
10 to 12 sun-dried tomatoes
2 ounces peas
4 ounces lobster meat
Cognac
2 ounces fresh lobster base
5 ounces cream
1 tablespoon butter
Chopped parsley and diced tomatoes for garnish
Salt and pepper to taste

Dredge lobster tail in flour. Sauté in olive oil; turn over. Add shallots and basil leaves. Add sun-dried tomatoes, peas, and lobster meat. Flambé with cognac. Add lobster base; reduce liquid. Add cream; reduce liquid. Add butter and allow to melt.

Garnish lobster tail with chopped parsley and diced tomatoes. Season with salt and pepper to taste.

Makes 1 serving.

Ferraro's

Recipient of the 1996 "Five Star Diamond Award"
from the American Academy of Hospitality Sciences

Penne Pasta with Pesto Sauce, Shrimp, and Shiitake Mushrooms

Kathleen McLaughlin, Chef

Pesto Sauce:
1½ cups fresh basil leaves
4 whole garlic cloves
½ cup fresh Italian parsley leaves, washed
¼ cup pine nuts, lightly toasted
6 tablespoons extra virgin olive oil
3 drops Tabasco® Pepper Sauce
1 teaspoon fresh lemon juice

In a food processor, blend all the Pesto Sauce ingredients. Set aside.

Penne Pasta with Shrimp and Mushrooms:
¾ pound penne pasta
3 tablespoons extra virgin olive oil
1 pound whole shrimp, shelled and deveined
4 ounces fresh shiitake mushrooms, sliced
6 tablespoons parmesan cheese, freshly-grated
Salt and pepper to taste
Italian parsley sprigs for garnish

Cook the pasta in boiling, salted water with 1 tablespoon olive oil until al dente. Reserve 4 tablespoons of the water.

In a large frying pan, sauté shrimp and mushrooms in remaining 2 tablespoons olive oil. Add the cooked pasta, reserved 4 tablespoons of water, and the Pesto Sauce. Toss well.

Fold in the grated parmesan cheese; add salt and pepper to taste. Garnish with fresh, crisp sprigs of Italian parsley.

Makes 4 main course servings or 8 appetizer servings.

BACCHANAL

Bacchanal
Caesars Palace
"Festival of Entertainment"

Sizzling Shrimp

1 to 2 tablespoons butter
28 large shrimp
¼ cup flour
4 tablespoons garlic, chopped
2 teaspoons shallots, chopped
9 ounces white wine
4 ounces lemon juice
1 teaspoon parsley, chopped
2 ounces chicken broth
8 ounces butter
2 ounces bell peppers, sliced
2 ounces mushrooms, sliced
4 ounces onions, sliced

Melt 1 to 2 tablespoons of butter in a skillet. Dust the shrimp with flour; sauté in melted butter until shrimp are brown on both sides. Add chopped garlic and shallots; sauté for ½ minute. Add white wine, lemon juice, and parsley. Let the sauce reduce for 1 minute. Add the chicken broth and 8 ounces of butter. Allow sauce to simmer until the butter melts.

Mix together the bell peppers and mushrooms. Drop in boiling water for 30 seconds; drain. Sauté the onion slices in a hot skillet and add the bell peppers and mushrooms. Pour the sauce and shrimp over the mixture of bell peppers, onions, and mushrooms. Serve with rice, sprinkled with parsley for color.

Makes 4 servings.

Kristofer's Steak House
Riviera Hotel & Casino
"Featuring Fine Steaks and Seafood with Fixed Prices"

Mongolian Beef

Stephen Chow, Chef

2 tablespoons cooking oil
12 ounces sirloin beef
6 ounces white onion, sliced
1 teaspoon ground, fresh garlic
2 tablespoons black soy sauce
1 tablespoon cooking wine
2 ounces bamboo shoot strips
4 ounces green bell pepper strips
4 to 5 tablespoons chicken broth
2 tablespoons hoison sauce
2 tablespoons hot bean sauce
1 tablespoon cornstarch/water mixture
2 ounces sliced water chestnuts
Few drops sesame seed oil

Heat wok and add cooking oil. Add sirloin beef, onion, and garlic. Stir fry for 1 minute. Add black soy sauce and cooking wine. Add bamboo shoots and green bell pepper; stir fry for another minute.

Add chicken broth and bring to a boil. Add hoison sauce, hot bean sauce, and 1 tablespoon cornstarch/water mixture. Add water chestnuts; stir fry about 1 minute. Add a few drops of sesame oil and stir in. Serve hot.

Makes 2 servings.

Osso Buco over Spinach Fettuccine

4 16-ounce veal shanks
1 medium bunch of celery, diced
2 medium white onions, diced
3 medium carrots, diced
1 pound button mushrooms, diced
1 medium bulb garlic, finely chopped
1 pound plum tomatoes
1 branch fresh rosemary
1 branch fresh sage
6 leaves fresh basil
1 cup extra virgin olive oil
Pinch of salt
Pinch of pepper
2 cups Chardonnay wine
1 quart chicken stock

1. Clean and peel white onions, celery, carrots, and garlic.
2. Dice celery, white onions, carrots, and mushrooms into ¼-inch cubes; set aside in bowl.
3. Finely chop garlic and place in vegetable-mixture bowl.
4. Cube plum tomatoes into ½-inch squares; set aside in separate bowl.
5. Finely chop the rosemary, sage, and basil; set aside in separate bowl.
6. Place olive oil into a sauce pot and sauté the vegetables from steps 2 and 3 over medium heat until the vegetables are golden.
7. Remove the vegetables from the oil and place on the side for future use.
8. Season the veal with salt and pepper.
9. Add veal shanks to sauce pot; bring heat to high and brown the veal.

10. Add cooked vegetables to pot with the veal. Add Chardonnay wine, chicken stock, and tomatoes; stir to mix.
11. Bring to boil for 2 minutes; lower heat to medium.
12. Add spices to sauce pot; cover.
13. Place covered sauce pot in 350-degree oven and cook for 3½ hours.

Note: When fully cooked, veal should separate easily from the bone.

Pasta:
1 pound spinach fettuccine
1 gallon water
1 teaspoon salt
3 ounces butter
2 ounces parmesan cheese

In a stock pot, bring water and salt to a boil. Cook fettuccine for 9 minutes, stirring constantly so that fettuccine does not stick together. In a sauté pan, melt butter over high heat. Add fettuccine and toss to coat with butter. Sprinkle with parmesan cheese, if desired. Serve hot.

Makes 4 servings.

Cafe Michelle West
"The Finest Euro-Merican Cuisine"

Penne Pasta with Veal and Red Pepper Pesto Sauce

Lucio Arancibia, Chef

Red Pepper Pesto Sauce:
4 fresh roasted red peppers, minced
1 cup parmesan cheese
1 ounce garlic
1 tablespoon parsley, minced
Pinch of basil
4 ounces walnuts
½ cup olive oil
1 ounce sun-dried tomatoes

Blend all ingredients until coarse. Set aside.

Penne Pasta with Veal:
8 ounces veal loin, cut into 1¼-ounce strips
¼ cup butter
3 ounces shallots, chopped
2 teaspoons minced garlic
1 tablespoon fresh thyme leaves
1 pinch paprika
½ cup white wine (a good Chardonnay)
1 cup fresh, ripe tomatoes (peeled, seedless), diced
1 quart cream or half and half
3 ounces fresh pea pods, julienned
16 ounces penne pasta
¼ cup olive oil
½ cup parmesan cheese

Sauté veal loin strips in butter until tender; set aside. In the same pan, cook shallots, garlic, thyme leaves, and paprika. Add the white wine; reduce. Add fresh tomatoes and cook 4 to 5 minutes. Add cream; reduce and strain.

Blanch pea pods in boiling water for 1 minute. Strain and set aside.

Cook penne pasta until al dente; strain. In a large skillet, sauté pasta in olive oil. Add veal, pea pods, parmesan cheese, and Red Pepper Pesto Sauce. Toss, garnish, and serve hot.

Makes 4 servings.

Camelot

Excalibur Hotel & Casino
"Gourmet Dining Fit for The King"

Indonesian-Style Lamb Chops

Eric Scuiller, Chef

8 lamb chops

Marinade:
1 cup salad oil
1 tablespoon dry mustard
2 tablespoons curry
1 tablespoon fresh oregano, minced
1 tablespoon fresh thyme, minced
1 tablespoon fresh cilantro, minced
2 garlic cloves, minced
4 bay leaves
1 teaspoon dry ground coriander
½ teaspoon ground cumin
¼ cup honey
¼ apple cider vinegar
Salt and pepper to taste

Mix all ingredients together in a medium-sized bowl. Place lamb chops in a large, separate bowl or a baking pan. Pour the marinade over the chops, making sure it gets in between them. Refrigerate, covered, for 1 hour.

Peanut Sauce:
2 tablespoons peanut oil
4 to 6 whole red Japanese peppers
½ teaspoon onion, minced
1 teaspoon ginger root, grated
3 tablespoons soy sauce
1 tablespoon worcestershire sauce (preferably Lea & Perrins)
Juice of ½ fresh lemon
½ cup coconut milk
¼ cup chicken stock

1 cup peanut butter

Heat a heavy-duty pan or a teflon pan. Add the peanut oil and quickly sauté the red peppers in it. Remove red peppers and set aside.

In the same pan, sauté the onion and ginger root until the onion is translucent. Add the soy sauce, worcestershire sauce, lemon juice, coconut milk, and chicken stock. Bring to a gentle boil; simmer about 2 minutes. Add the peanut butter and remove from heat. Mix well and set aside.

Lamb Chops:
Cook on a broiler or barbeque grill. Baste often with Peanut Sauce.

Note: This dish may be served with steamed rice. Place the steamed rice on a plate, arrange the lamb chops, and drizzle with peanut sauce. Serve hot.

Makes 8 servings.

Sterling Brunch
Bally's Las Vegas
Voted "Best Brunch in Las Vegas"

Beef with Black Mushrooms and Bamboo Shoots

1½ pounds flank steak
4 ounces vegetable oil
4 ounces white onions, sliced
1 cup chicken broth
4 ounces oyster sauce
4 ounces cornstarch
4 ounces snow peas
4 ounces soy sauce
2 ounces chicken powder
8 ounces bamboo shoots
½ pound black mushrooms
½ cup sugar
4 pinches salt

Cut the flank steak on an angle, about ⅛-inch thick. Set aside.

Heat wok with oil. Add the white onions and the flank steak. Cook for a few minutes in the hot wok. Add the chicken broth and let simmer for 5 minutes. Add cornstarch to thicken. Add the snow peas, soy sauce, chicken powder, bamboo shoots, black mushrooms, sugar, and salt. Cook a few more minutes, stirring constantly. Serve with steamed rice.

Makes 4 servings.

Rik' Shaw Chinese Cuisine
Riviera Hotel & Casino
"Some of the Finest Authentic Chinese Cuisine in Las Vegas!"

Saltimbocca alla Romana

A. Giovanni Vancheri, Chef

1 pound veal scallops, thinly-sliced and gently pounded
1 or 2 whole sage leaves, fresh or dried
½ pound Italian proscuitto ham, thinly-sliced
2 tablespoons butter
¼ cup extra virgin olive oil
Salt and freshly ground pepper to taste
1 cup dry white wine

Top each veal scallop with 1 or 2 sage leaves and a slice of proscuitto ham. Secure sage and ham with a toothpick. Brown veal scallops in hot butter and olive oil. Add salt and freshly ground pepper. Add white wine; reduce heat and simmer for about 5 minutes. Transfer veal scallops to warmed plate. Remove toothpicks.

Increase heat and boil the pan juices until reduced by half. Pour over veal scallops and proscuitto ham. Serve immediately with vegetable of your choice.

Makes 1 to 2 servings.

Café Milano
ITALIAN RISTORANTE

Gio's Cafe Milano
Recipient of "Best of the Best Five Star Diamond Award"

Pappardelle with Lamb Osso Buco

Vladimir Reitmaier, Chef

10 1-pound lamb shanks
4 ounces olive oil
Salt and black pepper to taste
8 bay leaves
5 garlic cloves, crushed
1 pound large carrots, diced
1 pound large celery stalks, diced
1 pound large onions, diced
25 ounces dry red wine
32 ounces veal or beef stock
1 teaspoon thyme
Egg noodles (pappardelle), cooked
Romano cheese, grated as needed
Gremolada garnish: 2 parts Italian parsley, 1 part garlic, 2 parts lemon zest

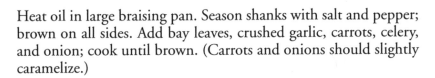

Heat oil in large braising pan. Season shanks with salt and pepper; brown on all sides. Add bay leaves, crushed garlic, carrots, celery, and onion; cook until brown. (Carrots and onions should slightly caramelize.)

Deglaze with red wine and let reduce by half. Add veal or beef stock and thyme. Cook slowly 1½ hours; reserve.

For each serving, heat 1 shank with 4 ounces of sauce. Add desired amount of cooked egg noodles. Top with sauce and heat through. Season with grated romano and gremolada garnish. Serve in hot pasta bowl.

Makes 10 servings.

Blue Diamond Buffet
Boomtown Hotel & Casino
"Boomtown, Best of the West"

Steak Sicilian

2 12-ounce New York Strip steaks, trimmed of fat
1 tablespoon fresh garlic, chopped
¾ cup olive oil
1 level teaspoon dried, crushed oregano
½ teaspoon salt
¼ teaspoon black pepper, ground
1 level teaspoon dried, crushed basil

Preheat oven to 400 degrees. In a 1-quart bowl, mix garlic, olive oil, oregano, salt, black pepper, and basil to form a marinade. Set aside for 20 minutes.

In a baking pan, place the 2 steaks approximately 2 inches apart. Pour marinade onto steaks and bake (medium rare: 10-12 minutes; medium: 12-14 minutes; well done: 15-16 minutes). Remove from oven and discard excess oil in bottom of pan. Remove steaks and place on platter with baked potato or vegetables of your choice.

Makes 2 servings.

STARBOARD TACK

Starboard Jack

"Mulberry Street-Style Cooking Comes to Las Vegas. The Tack is Back!"

Fettuccine con Porcini Funghi

Piero Broglia, Chef

1½ pounds porcini mushrooms (fresh or fresh-frozen)
1 teaspoon mushroom base
1 cup tomato sauce
Cornstarch as needed
1 teaspoon olive oil
1 teaspoon garlic, ground
2 teaspoons red onions, minced
1 pinch crushed red chilies
2 pinches fresh basil
Splash of white wine
5 ounces fettuccine

Porcini Sauce:
Boil mushrooms for 3 minutes in enough water to cover them.
Remove from water; drain and cool. (Reserve mushroom stock.)
Slice mushrooms; set aside. Add mushroom base to the mushroom
stock. Stir in tomato sauce. Thicken mixture with cornstarch.

In olive oil, sauté garlic, red onions, and red chilies for 2 minutes.
Add basil and sliced mushrooms; sauté for 1 minute. Add a splash
of white wine. Pour in mushroom base/tomato sauce mixture and
allow to simmer.

Fettuccine:
Add 5 ounces fettuccine to boiling water and cook until al dente;
drain. Add 8 ounces Porcini Sauce to pasta. Sauté for 1 minute.
Arrange in a bowl and garnish with parsley.

Makes 4 servings.

Chef Piero's al Dente
Bally's Las Vegas
"A New Flavor of Light Italian Dining"

Angel Hair with Arugula and Artichokes

Ray San Sota, Chef

1 pound angel hair (capellini) pasta
2 bunches arugula leaves
1 head broccoli, cut into small florets
12 snow peas, trimmed
8 whole baby artichoke hearts, quartered
6 ounces plus 1 ounce olive oil
4 teaspoons garlic, chopped
Salt and pepper to taste
2 tablespoons fresh tarragon, chopped
½ pound parmesan cheese, grated
4 ounces chicken stock or bouillon

Cook pasta for 4 to 5 minutes in 6 quarts of boiling, salted water. Drain, cool, and set aside.

Sauté arugula, broccoli, snow peas, and artichokes in 1 ounce of olive oil. Add chopped garlic; sauté briefly. Add salt and pepper to taste. Add tarragon and remaining olive oil.

Reheat pasta. Add to pan of vegetables; sprinkle with parmesan cheese. Add chicken stock. Stir all together and serve hot.

Makes 4 to 6 servings.

Andiamo
Las Vegas Hilton
"The Finest Flavors of the Mediterranean Coast"

Pasta Primavera

Maria Perri, Chef

6 ounces penne pasta
1 ounce fresh garlic, chopped
1 tablespoon olive oil
½ cup mushrooms
½ cup zucchini squash, cut into bite-sized pieces
½ cup broccoli, cut into bite-sized pieces
½ cup yellow squash, cut into bite-sized pieces
6 fresh snow peas
½ teaspoon salt or to taste
Pinch of white pepper
2 ounces chicken broth
4 ounces marinara sauce
½ cup roma tomatoes, cut into bite-sized pieces

Cook penne pasta until al dente; set aside. Sauté garlic in olive oil until golden brown. Add mushrooms, zucchini squash, broccoli, yellow squash, and snow peas. Add salt and white pepper. Sauté vegetables until tender-crisp.

Add chicken broth and marinara sauce. Simmer until blended thoroughly. Add roma tomatoes and hot penne pasta. Toss gently.

Makes 2 servings.

The Bootlegger Ristorante

"Romantic Italian Dining Since 1949,
Where Locals and Celebrities Gather in Las Vegas"

Pesto Sauce al Pomodoro

A. Giovanni Vancheri, Chef

20 basil leaves
1½ tablespoons chopped parsley
6 cloves garlic
6⅔ tablespoons extra virgin olive oil
7 ounces fresh tomatoes, cubed
Salt and black pepper to taste
2 tablespoons pine nuts
1 pound linguine
4¼ ounces mozzarella cheese, sliced into thin strips

Pound together the basil, parsley, and garlic with a mortar and pestle, or combine in a blender. While blending these ingredients, pour in the olive oil in a thin thread. Add salt and a pinch of black pepper. Add the pine nuts and blend all. When a thick sauce forms, mix in the cubed tomatoes.

Boil the linguine in salted water until al dente; drain. Transfer the linguine to a pasta bowl. Pour sauce over the linguine. Spread mozzarella strips over the top. Serve hot.

Makes 6 servings.

Café Milano
ITALIAN RISTORANTE

Gio's Café Milano
Recipient of "Best of the Best Five Star Diamond Award"

Portabella Squash Blossom Tamales

Thomas Birdwell, Chef

Masa:
3 tablespoons butter
3 tablespoons shortening
1 teaspoon toasted cumin
2 teaspoons salt
2 cups masa harina
4 medium-sized portabella mushrooms, sliced and sautéed
    with white onion slices
¼ cup water

Cream the butter and shortening. Add in toasted cumin, salt, and masa harina. Add sautéed portabella mushrooms. Mix in food processor until biscuit consistency. Drizzle the water into the mixture. (Mixture should have the same consistency as cookie dough.)

Filling:
1 tablespoon olive oil
4 medium-sized portabella mushrooms
2 cloves of garlic, chopped
1 shallot, chopped
6 squash blossoms, stemmed and sliced
Salt and pepper to taste
½ cup goat cheese
1 teaspoon fresh thyme, chopped

In the olive oil, sauté the portabella mushrooms with the garlic and shallot until just tender. Add in the sliced squash blossoms. Season with salt and pepper. When cool, add the goat cheese and mix in the thyme.

Portabella Cream:
½ cup onion, chopped
1 tablespoon olive oil
5 cloves roasted garlic
1 quart heavy cream
1 sprig thyme
1 bay leaf
3 sautéed portabella mushrooms
Salt and pepper to taste

Sauté the onion in olive oil. Add the roasted garlic, then the heavy cream. Add the thyme sprig and bay leaf; reduce liquid by ¾. After the liquid is reduced, remove and discard bay leaf and thyme sprig. Add sauteéd portabella mushrooms and blend mixture in blender. Season with salt and pepper to taste.

Makes 6 servings.

Coyote Cafe

Coyote Cafe
MGM Grand Hotel & Casino
"Have a Howlin' Good Day"

Spaghetti alla Siracusana

1 medium-sized eggplant
1 yellow bell pepper
2 salted anchovies
1 tablespoon capers
2 garlic cloves, crushed
½ cup extra virgin olive oil
Salt and pepper to taste
2 cups fresh, ripe tomatoes, diced
⅓ cup black olives
10 leaves fresh basil
Salt and pepper to taste
1 pound spaghetti
Percorino romano cheese, grated (optional)

Cut the eggplant into small pieces. Place on a plate and cover with salt; set aside for ½ hour.

Fill a medium-sized pot with water and bring to a boil.

Pass yellow bell pepper over a stove burner until its skin peels easily. Remove seeds and membrane and cut into thin pieces; set aside.

Wash salt from the anchovies and chop the capers; set aside. Sauté crushed garlic cloves in olive oil until oil is golden brown. Remove and discard the garlic.

To the olive oil, add the anchovies and allow them to melt. Rinse the salt off the eggplant, pat dry, and place in the pan to simmer. Add the diced tomatoes. After a few minutes, add the bell pepper, black olives, capers, and basil. Add salt and pepper to taste. Cook for about 20 minutes or until vegetables are done.

When the sauté pan's contents are half-cooked, place the spaghetti in the boiling water and add ½ teaspoon of salt. Cook until al dente. (Do not overcook.) Drain the spaghetti.

Place the spaghetti in the sauté pan with the sauce. Over medium heat, blend all ingredients together. Place spaghetti and sauce in serving dishes. Sprinkle fresh, grated percorino romano cheese on top, if desired. Serve hot.

Makes 4 servings.

Sergio's Italian Gardens Ristorante

Recipient of "Five Star Best of the Best Award"
and "Award of Excellence"

Risotto Agli Asparagie Porcini

Marco Di Tullio, Chef

4 ounces butter
3 ounces onion, chopped
6 ounces carnaroli rice
4 ounces white wine
24 ounces chicken stock
Salt and pepper
¼ ounce fresh herb combination
    (rosemary, sage, thyme, basil), chopped
4 ounces fresh porcini mushrooms
3 ounces fresh asparagus tips
1½ ounces parmesan cheese, grated
¼ ounce fresh Italian parsley, chopped

PRIMAVERA

In a large frying pan, sauté the onions in 1 ounce of butter until golden. Add the rice and let toast for 30 seconds. Add the white wine and stir continuously, using a wooden spoon.

Bring chicken stock to a boil. Add 12 ounces to the rice mixture. Stir until the chicken stock evaporates. Add the rest of the stock. Add salt and pepper to taste.

In a small frying pan, sauté the porcini mushrooms and asparagus tips in 1 ounce of butter. Add to the rice mixture. Add in the fresh herb combination and lower the heat.

After 20 minutes, turn off the heat. Add the remaining butter, the parmesan cheese, and the Italian parsley. Stir energetically for 30 seconds.

Serve in a large bowl, garnished with an Italian parsley leaf.

Makes 2 servings.

Primavera
Caesars Palace
"Creative Italian Cuisine"

Antipasti con Capellini

8 ounces angel hair pasta (capellini)
2 ounces olive oil
1 ounce mushrooms, sliced
1 ounce sun-dried tomatoes, diced
½ ounce olives, sliced
4 artichoke hearts
1 ounce salami, thinly sliced
1 pinch salt and pepper
1 pinch crushed red pepper
½ ounce parmesan cheese

Cook angel hair pasta until al dente; set aside. In a sauté pan, lightly sauté the mushrooms in olive oil. Add all other ingredients except pasta and parmesan cheese. Sauté lightly.

Place angel hair pasta in a large pasta bowl. Add in the other ingredients and toss together. Top with parmesan cheese and serve with salad and bread.

Makes 1 serving.

Strings Italian Cafe

"Pastatively the Best!"

Pasta della Casa

2 ounces lemon pepper oil
½ ounce roasted garlic
Vegetable purée: carrots, mushrooms, broccoli, spinach, red and green onions, and olive oil
2 ounces spaghetti sauce
1 ounce chicken stock
1 fresh basil leaf
1½ ounces artichoke hearts
1 ounce green bell peppers, cut into julienne strips
1 ounce red bell peppers, cut into julienne strips
1 ounce mushrooms, sliced
2 ounces tomatoes, chopped
8 ounces penne pasta, cooked al dente, then drained
1 ounce grated parmesan cheese

Heat lemon pepper oil in sauté pan. When oil is hot, add roasted garlic. Add vegetable purée, spaghetti sauce, chicken stock, and fresh basil. (These ingredients must be added in exact order.) Add artichoke hearts, green bell peppers, red bell peppers, mushrooms, and tomatoes. Heat through.

Add cooked and drained penne pasta. Toss in pan until completely mixed. Top with parmesan cheese. Serve hot.

Makes 1 serving.

Romano's Macaroni Grille
"All the Italian You Need to Know"

Grand Marnier Soufflé

Timothy J. Prescott, Chef

6 large eggs, separated
¾ cup granulated sugar
2 tablespoons unsalted butter, melted
1 teaspoon vanilla
¼ cup Grand Marnier liqueur
1 teaspoon orange zest
½ teaspoon ground nutmeg
Granulated sugar for dusting
2 ounces sweet white chocolate, melted
1 tablespoon powdered sugar

CREATIVE
CATERING

In a double boiler, whisk egg yolks and granulated sugar until the consistency of hollandaise sauce. (Whisk constantly but do not overcook.) Remove from heat. Very slowly, whisk in the melted butter, vanilla, Grand Marnier liqueur, orange zest, and nutmeg. Set aside.

In a 1-quart mixing bowl, beat the egg whites until peaks form. Fold the Grand Marnier mixture into the egg whites.

Heat oven to 375 degrees. Lightly grease 4 individual soufflé molds and dust with granulated sugar. Pour the Grand Marnier/egg whites mixture into each mold in equal parts. Bake for approximately 15 minutes. Remove from the oven; lace with the melted white chocolate. Sprinkle with powdered sugar.

Makes 4 servings.

Creative Catering

"We Design a Variety of Fine Foods for Your Special Occasion."

J-Sundae

Cindy Pawlcyn, Chef

½ cup Chocolate Sauce
2 cups pecans (Seasoned Nuts)
8 scoops vanilla ice cream
½ cup Butterscotch Sauce
⅓ cup whipped cream

Pour 1 tablespoon of Chocolate Sauce into each parfait or sundae glass and place 3 or 4 pecans and a scoop of ice cream on top. Pour a tablespoon of Butterscotch Sauce on the ice cream, followed by a tablespoon each of the Chocolate and Butterscotch Sauces, whipped cream, and 2 or 3 pecans.

Seasoned Nuts:
2 cups raw, shelled nuts (pecans, walnut halves, almonds, hazelnuts, pistachios, or peanuts)
1 quart water
½ to ¾ cup powdered sugar
3 cups peanut oil
Kosher salt or sea salt

If the nuts have skins that are easily removed, rub off the skins. Place the nuts in a pan with the water and bring to a boil. Remove from heat, drain, and immediately coat the nuts thoroughly with powdered sugar. Heat the oil to 375 degrees in a deep-fryer or cast-iron skillet; fry the nuts until golden and crisp. (Do not over-crowd while frying.) Drain the nuts on a cookie sheet or in a colander. (Do not drain them on paper towels as they will stick.) While the nuts are still hot, sprinkle them with salt to taste.

Chocolate Sauce:
8 ounces semisweet chocolate (preferably Guittard's French Vanilla)

½ cup unsalted butter
2 tablespoons brandy or cognac
1 tablespoon triple sec
¾ cup light corn syrup
¾ cup heavy cream

Cut the chocolate and butter into small pieces and place with the brandy, triple sec, and corn syrup in a double boiler and allow to soften. (The butter will melt, but the chocolate chunks will hold their shape until pressed.) Remove from the heat and whisk together. When the mixture is smooth, stir in the heavy cream.

Butterscotch Sauce:
5 tablespoons unsalted butter
¾ cup light brown sugar
¾ cup dark brown sugar
1 cup light corn syrup
1 cup heavy cream

Combine the butter, sugars, and corn syrup in a saucepan; bring to a rolling boil. (The mixture should get a little darker as it cooks.) Stir in the heavy cream; return to a boil, and then remove from heat. This is best served warm.

"No crybabies"

White Russian Granita Complemented by Chocolate Hazelnut Biscotti

Terence Fong, Chef

White Russian Granita:
2½ cups water
½ cup sugar
3¾ teaspoons instant espresso powder
1½ tablespoons dark corn syrup
½ cup heavy cream
¼ cup vodka
¼ cup kahlua
½ teaspoon cinnamon
Chocolate shavings and whipped cream for garnish

Bring water and sugar to a boil; remove from heat. Add remaining ingredients and mix well.

Pour mixture into a cake pan, 10 x 13 inches, and freeze. Stir every 4 hours to break up ice crystals. Spoon into serving dishes and top with whipped cream. Serve with Chocolate Hazelnut Biscotti.

Chocolate Hazelnut Biscotti:
2 eggs
2 tablespoons vegetable oil
1 teaspoon vanilla extract
1½ cups all-purpose flour
¾ cup sugar
⅓ cup Dutch cocoa powder, packed
1 teaspoon baking powder

¼ teaspoon salt
⅓ cup hazelnuts, chopped

Heat oven to 350 degrees. In mixer with paddle attachment, combine eggs, vegetable oil, and vanilla extract. In a separate bowl, sift together flour, sugar, cocoa powder, baking powder, and salt. Add to egg mixture just until fully incorporated. Fold in hazelnuts. Wrap dough in cellophane and refrigerate for 2 hours.

On a floured surface, divide dough into 3 parts and form into logs. Bake on an oiled baking sheet just until centers are firm.

Remove biscotti from oven and cool slightly. Slice at an angle to make cookies. Reduce oven heat to 250 degrees. Return biscotti to oven and bake for a few minutes until crisp.

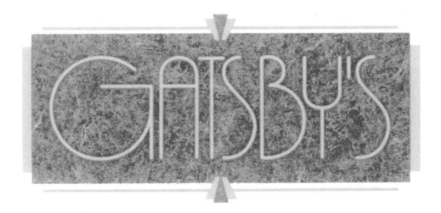

Gatsby's
MGM Grand Hotel & Casino
"Setting a New Standard for a Special Blend
of the Finest Euro-Asian Cuisine"

White Chocolate Cheesecake

Crust:
1½ cups graham cracker crumbs
¼ pound melted butter

Mix together well and set aside.

Filling:
1¼ pounds cream cheese
5 ounces granulated sugar
4 ounces sour cream
5 whole eggs
1 teaspoon lemon juice
1 teaspoon vanilla extract
Dash salt
8 ounces white chocolate chips

Heat oven to 325 degrees. Combine the cream cheese and sugar; mix until smooth. Add sour cream, eggs, lemon juice, vanilla extract, and salt; blend well. Melt white chocolate in double boiler. Add to the cream cheese mixture and blend until free of lumps.

Grease a 10-inch cake pan. Press graham-cracker-crumb mixture onto the bottom until firm. Spread cream cheese mixture over graham-cracker-crumb mixture. Place cake pan on a rimmed cookie sheet.

Place cookie sheet in oven and fill with water. Bake cheesecake for 1 hour. Remove from oven and allow to cool on a rack for 5 hours. Refrigerate overnight. Using a small knife, carefully free edges of cheesecake to release from cake pan.

Binion's Ranch House
Binion's Horseshoe Hotel & Casino
"Steaks as World Famous as the Gambling"

Strawberries Flambé

Melt 3 pats of butter. Add brown sugar. Squeeze ½ of an orange over the brown sugar. Flambé with cherry brandy.

Add cream of strawberry liqueur. Add fresh strawberries and allow them to cook. Flambé with dark rum and Grand Marnier.

Pour over vanilla ice cream.

The Burgundy Room
Lady Luck Casino & Hotel
"Fine Dining in Elegant Surroundings"

English Trifle

1 4½-ounce package vanilla pudding and pie filling mix
2 cups light cream
1½ cups heavy cream
3 tablespoons sugar
2 tablespoons red raspberry preserves
1 10-inch round sponge cake
¼ cup dark Puerto Rican rum
¼ cup dry sherry
1½ cups frozen raspberries
Fresh raspberries for decoration

In a medium pan, combine pudding mix and light cream. Cook, stirring constantly until mixture comes to a boil and thickens; chill. Whip ½ cup heavy cream and 1 tablespoon sugar until stiff. Fold into chilled pudding mixture.

Coat the inside of a deep 10-inch bowl with raspberry preserves to within 1 inch of the top. Slice sponge cake horizontally into fourths. Place top slice crust-side-up in bottom of bowl, curving edges of cake upward. Combine rum and sherry. Sprinkle about 2 tablespoons of the rum/sherry mixture over the cake slice. Spread ⅓ of the chilled pudding mixture over the cake slice. Sprinkle ½ cup frozen raspberries over the pudding mixture.

Repeat procedure twice. Cover with remaining cake layer, crust side down. Sprinkle with remaining rum/sherry mixture.

Whip remaining 1 cup heavy cream and 2 tablespoons sugar until stiff. Place whipped cream/sugar mixture in pastry bag with fluted tip. Pipe rosettes around the edge of the bowl and in the center.

Decorate with fresh raspberries. Chill at least 8 hours. Spoon onto chilled dessert plates.

Makes 12 servings.

Lawry's The Prime Rib

"For the Prime of Your Life"

Bananas Foster

1 tablespoon butter
½ cup brown sugar
1 ounce rum
1 ounce banana liqueur
1 ounce Frangelico® liqueur
2 bananas, sliced
4 scoops vanilla ice cream

Melt the butter. Add brown sugar and whisk over medium heat for approximately 30 seconds until the mixture forms a paste. Add the rum, banana liqueur, and Frangelico® liqueur; flambé. Whisk for an additional 30 seconds. Add sliced bananas and cook for 1 additional minute.

Note: Do not overcook the bananas.

Spoon the mixture over ice cream and serve.

Makes 1 serving.

Treasure Island at the Mirage

GLOSSARY

Achiote: Small, reddish seeds; often used in Caribbean cooking.

Aioli: A type of mayonnaise made with oil, eggs, lemon juice, and flavorings.

Al dente: To cook until "barely tender," the ideal consistency for pasta.

Aquavit: A clear, Scandinavian liqueur flavored with caraway seeds.

Arugula: A pungent Italian salad herb.

Béarnaise sauce: A sauce made with red wine vinegar, green onion, butter, egg yolks, and herbs.

Biscotti: A twice-baked Italian biscuit often dipped into dessert wine or coffee.

Blanch: To plunge fruits or vegetables briefly into boiling water to loosen skins and enhance color and flavor.

Bordelaise sauce: A meat sauce made with beef broth, red wine, flour, butter, onion, and herbs.

Braise: To brown meat in fat, then cook, tightly covered, in a small amount of liquid for a lengthy period in order to tenderize and enhance flavor.

Brunoise: To cut into very small pieces ($\frac{1}{8}$-inch dice); to garnish as such.

Bouillabaise: A fish chowder; originally from the Mediterranean area.

Butterfly: To remove heads and shells (but not tails) from shrimp; shrimp is cut deep, almost to underside, before vein is removed and shrimp is pressed open.

Cayenne: A hot red pepper powder made from seeds and pods.

Chablis: A dry, white burgundy wine from France.

Chambord: A raspberry liqueur.

Chardonnay: A dry, versatile wine; sometimes called Pinot Chardonnay.

Chervil: A plant from the parsley family; leaves are used to flavor foods.

Chorizo: A hot, peppery Spanish pork or beef sausage.

Cilantro (coriander): A lacy parsley used to flavor salsas and sauces.

Cognac: A fine French brandy.

Court bouillon: Seasoned liquid; usually used for poaching fish.

Deglaze: To swirl liquid in a pan to dissolve cooked particles on bottom.

Dredge: To cover or coat food with flour or cornmeal.

Egg wash: Beaten egg mixed with a small amount of water; mixture is brushed onto breads and other foods before they are baked.

Emulsify: To blend two unmixable liquids, such as oil and water or vinegar.

Escargot: An edible snail, usually served in the shell.

Espresso: A strong, Italian-roast coffee.

Fillet (filet): A piece of boneless meat, fish, or poultry.

Flambé (flame): To ignite warmed alcoholic beverages poured over food.

Foie gras: A term generally applied to duck or goose liver.

Frangelico®: Trade name for a hazelnut-flavored liqueur from Italy.

Gelatin leaf: Paper-thin sheets of gelatin; used in place of granulated gelatin.

Grand Marnier: Trade name for a fine orange-flavored liqueur from France.

Gravel sugar: Coarse-textured sugar (sugar crystals); less sweet than granulated.

Gremolada (gremolata): An Italian garnish generally made with minced parsley, lemon peel, and ground garlic.

Hollandaise sauce: A sauce made with egg yolks, lemon juice, and butter.

Hoisin sauce: A Chinese sauce made of soybeans and seasonings.

Kahlua: A coffee-flavored liqueur.

Julienne: To cut into matchstick-size pieces.

Lump crab: The large, select pieces of meat from the crab shell.

Madeira: A strong, semi-sweet white or amber wine from Portugal.

Marsala: A sweet to semi-dry wine from Sicily.

Masa harina: A wheat and corn flour blend; used in Mexican fare.

Mince: To cut into very small pieces.

Mortar and pestle: A bowl-shaped container and batlike instrument used as a pair for grinding and pulverizing herbs, spices, and other foods.

Orange roughy: A lowfat, white New Zealand fish with a mild flavor.

Pancetta: A moist, distinctive Italian version of bacon.

Pesto: A sauce made from oil, garlic, basil, parmesan, and pine nuts.

Phyllo (filo): Thin "leaves" of pastry dough.

Plantain: A tropical banana plant yielding a fruit eaten as a cooked vegetable.

Poblano: A large chile with a mild to medium-hot flavor.

Porcinis: Italian mushrooms with a slight hazelnut flavor.

Port: A sweet, heavy-bodied, dark red wine; originally from Portugal.

Portabellas: Large, flavorful mushrooms.

Prawns: A term used, traditionally on the West Coast, for large shrimp.

Puff pastry: A French pastry made by layering dough and butter; dough separates into flaky layers as it bakes, after which it is generally sliced and filled.

Purée: To blend into a smooth, thick mixture.

Ragout: A thick, highly seasoned stew.

Reduce: To decrease liquid volume by boiling rapidly in an uncovered pan.

Sauté: To fry quickly in a small amount of oil or butter.

Sauterne: A golden, dry-to-sweet, full-bodied wine; originally from France.

Shallot: A round or elongated member of the onion family.

Sherry: A fortified yellow-to-gold wine from Spain.

Shiitake: A large, versatile, dark mushroom; originally from Japan and Korea.

Simmer: To cook in liquid over low heat while bubbles form and collapse.

Simple syrup: Syrup formed by cooking sugar slowly in water or fruit juice.

Soba: Long, thin, flat noodles, usually made of whole wheat and buckwheat.

Tamale: Corn mush spread on corn husk; filled, rolled, tied, and steamed.

Tartare: A mayonnaise-like sauce made with oil, hard-cooked egg, and herbs.

Tomato concassé: Tomatoes that are peeled, seeded, and chopped coarsely.

Triple sec: A strong, orange-flavored liqueur, such as Cointreau.

Vinaigrette: A dressing or sauce made from olive oil, vinegar, and seasonings.

Walnut oil: A salad oil made from pressed walnut meats.

Zest: Grated, colored outer peel of oranges, lemons and limes.

INDEX

About the Editor

Linda Linssen received a Bachelor of Science degree in Language Arts Education from Southwest State University in Marshall, Minnesota, and completed graduate courses at Bread Loaf School of English in Middlebury, Vermont, and Santa Fe, New Mexico. She taught secondary English and Creative Writing in Granite Falls, Minnesota, before moving to Las Vegas, Nevada, in 1993. In Las Vegas she works as a freelance copywriter and teaches writing courses part-time at the Community College of Southern Nevada. Cooking is her avocation.